Questions and Answers About

FRESHWATER
ANIMALS

MICHAEL CHINERY

ILLUSTRATED BY WAYNE FORD
AND ERIC ROBSON

Kingfisher Books

NEW YORK

KINGFISHER BOOKS
Grisewood & Dempsey Inc.
95 Madison Avenue
New York, New York 10016

First American edition 1994
10 9 8 7 6 5 4 3 2 1 (lib. bdg.)
10 9 8 7 6 5 4 3 2 1 (pbk.)

Library of Congress Cataloging-in-Publication Data
Chinery, Michael.
    Questions and answers about freshwater animals / by
Michael Chinery; illustrated by Wayne Ford and Eric
Robson. – 1st American ed.
        p. cm.
    Includes index.
    1. Freshwater fauna – Miscellanea – Juvenile
literature. [1. Freshwater animals.] I. Ford, Wayne, ill.
II. Robson, Eric, ill. III. Title. IV. Title: Freshwater
animals.
QL141.C48 1994
591.92'9 – dc20 93-29415 CIP AC

ISBN 1-85697-973-3 (lib. bdg.)
ISBN 1-85697-962-8 (pbk.)

Series editor: Mike Halson
Series designer: Terry Woodley
Designer: Dave West Children's Books
Illustrators: Wayne Ford (pp. 1, 10–12, 15–17, 20–21,
26–28, 30–31, 36–37); Eric Robson (pp. 2–9, 13–14,
18–19, 22–25, 29, 32–35, 38)
Cover illustrations: John Butler

Printed in Hong Kong

CONTENTS

Where do freshwater animals live?

The Earth's fresh waters consist of rivers, streams, lakes, and ponds. They take up only a small part of the Earth's surface, but the creatures that live in and around fresh water are very important. There are over 8,000 kinds of freshwater fish alone—about two-fifths of all the fish species. Frogs, toads, newts, and salamanders are found in all parts of the world. Lakes, ponds, and marshes are the chief freshwater habitats of birds, many of them feeding on the insect population. Wherever there is fresh water there are freshwater animals.

DO YOU KNOW

Waterfalls usually occur where rivers flow from hard rocks onto softer ones. The running water wears the softer rock away more quickly and leaves the hard rock standing up like a cliff with the river crashing noisily over it.

Grebe

A lake forms where a river flows down into a hollow area. The river eventually finds its way out and continues its journey to the sea. All kinds of fish live in the lake and ospreys hunt them from the air. Grebes and other water birds live around the water's edge.

Mountain streams are cold and rocky and are usually too fast for fish to live in them. Farther down the valley the current is slower, and this is where the salmon comes to lay its eggs. Sticklebacks swim here too, and dippers nest along the water's edge.

Salmon

The stretch of river nearest the sea is called the estuary. The water is salty here. Flocks of wading birds visit the muddy banks uncovered at low tide to feed on worms and shell-fish. Otters hunt for eels and other fish in quiet estuaries.

Otter

The river flows slowly through the lowlands in great loops. Eels and many other fish swim here, but they are not easy to see in the muddy water. Swans nest on the river banks, while dragonflies dart through the air.

Dragonfly

DO YOU KNOW

The animals that live in the calm or still waters of lakes and ponds are similar to those of slow-moving rivers. Frogs and newts breed there in the spring, and so do ducks and moorhens.

Does a hippopotamus have enemies?

The hippopotamus is the world's biggest freshwater animal. It weighs up to 4 tons and, although it is a plant eater, it is a very dangerous creature. An adult hippopotamus can pick up a crocodile and bite it in half. Hippos live in groups in and around the rivers of Africa. The adults have no enemies, but crocodiles often eat baby hippos. When people killed the crocodiles in one area the hippo population grew so much that they ate all the crops!

HIPPO FACTS

• Hippopotamus means "river horse," but the hippo is actually a huge pig, up to 13 feet long and about 5 feet high. The male's tusks can be over 3 feet long.

• An adult hippo will eat about 450 pounds of grass and other plants in a single night.

Male hippos fight with their tusks, which can cause terrible injuries. The hippos often die from their wounds.

Hippos come out of the water to graze on land at night. They often destroy farm crops. They also eat lots of water plants.

Oxpeckers commonly perch on hippos on the riverbank. They eat the bloodsucking ticks and flies that attack the hippos.

? DO YOU KNOW

The hippo's skin is kept clean by a type of small fish. The fish even cleans the hippo's teeth for it.

The hippo can walk or run along the riverbed for over 4 minutes without having to come up for air.

When resting in the river by day, the hippopotamus raises just its eyes, ears, and nostrils above the water.

How does the water strider get its name?

The water strider is an insect that lives on the surface of ponds and slow-moving streams. It "strides" across the water with its long middle legs and preys on small insects that fall onto the surface.

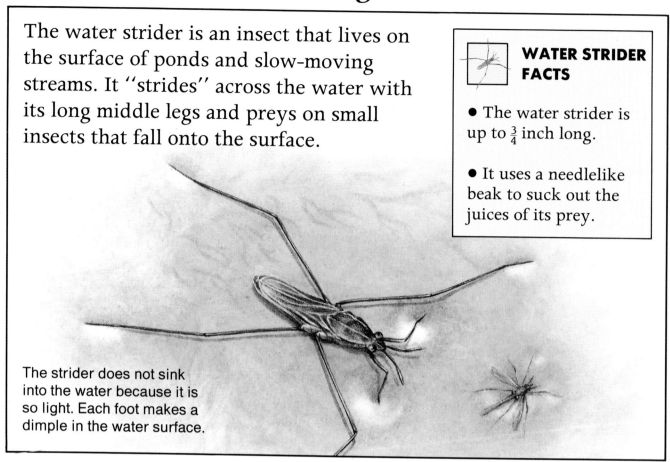

The strider does not sink into the water because it is so light. Each foot makes a dimple in the water surface.

WATER STRIDER FACTS

● The water strider is up to $\frac{3}{4}$ inch long.

● It uses a needlelike beak to suck out the juices of its prey.

When does a raft spider go hunting?

The raft spider spends most of its time on the surface of small pools. It usually rests on a floating leaf or twig. When the spider feels the vibrations of an insect or a small fish, it darts off to catch and eat it.

SURVIVAL WATCH

Raft spiders almost died out in Britain when the swamp that was their home began to dry up. New pools were dug to save them.

The raft spider's feet rest on the water surface. They pick up vibrations that tell the spider that food might be nearby.

Why does a dipper dip?

The dipper gets its name from its habit of bobbing up and down for food while standing on rocks in fast-flowing streams. It also spends up to two hours every day walking or swimming under the water. It eats all kinds of small water creatures, but freshwater shrimps are its favorite food. Dippers live by upland rivers in many parts of the Northern Hemisphere. They nest among waterside rocks and trees.

DIPPER FACTS

● Dippers are 7 inches long and weigh about 3 ounces. They can eat their own weight of food in a day.

● Dipper chicks can dive and swim before they can fly.

The dipper's eyes are specially constructed so that the birds can see just as well in the water as they can in the air.

The dipper often runs along the streambed as it searches for food. It can also swim very well by flapping its wings.

9

How do beavers build their homes?

Beavers live by rivers in the forests of North America and Europe. They are wonderful builders and are famous for the dams that they build across streams. They usually build their homes, called lodges, in the ponds that form behind the dams. There they are safe from most of their enemies. Some beavers live in burrows in the riverbank instead of in lodges, but the burrows still have underwater entrances. Beavers live in family groups of about 12, and all the animals help with the work.

SURVIVAL WATCH

Beavers became rare in the 1800s, when many thousands were killed for their fine fur. They are now protected and have become quite common again in some areas.

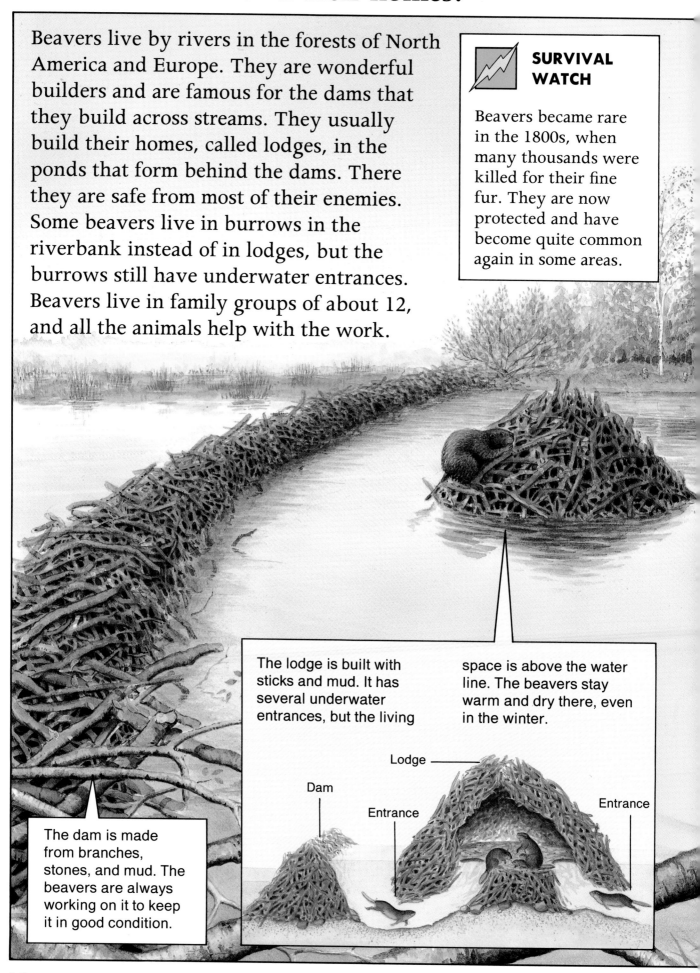

The lodge is built with sticks and mud. It has several underwater entrances, but the living space is above the water line. The beavers stay warm and dry there, even in the winter.

The dam is made from branches, stones, and mud. The beavers are always working on it to keep it in good condition.

Lodge

Dam

Entrance

Entrance

BEAVER FACTS

● The beaver is 3½ feet long from nose to tail and weighs 65 pounds. Its back feet are webbed for swimming.

● When a beaver spots an enemy, such as a wolf or a puma, it slaps the water with its tail. The sound, heard up to half a mile away, warns other beavers of the danger.

Beavers are strong swimmers and can stay underwater for 15 minutes. Dense, oily fur keeps their bodies dry and warm.

Beavers cut down trees with their sharp teeth. They eat the tender young shoots and use the rest to build with.

The broad tail is used for steering in the water. On land, it forms a sort of seat while the beaver gnaws the trees.

11

Which fish breathe air?

Several kinds of lungfish live in tropical rivers. Their gills are not very efficient and they surface now and then to gulp air into simple lungs. Some lungfish drown if they can't get to the surface. Scientists think that some kinds of lungfish left the water millions of years ago and developed into the first newtlike amphibians. Lungfish feed mainly on water snails, which they crush with big flat teeth.

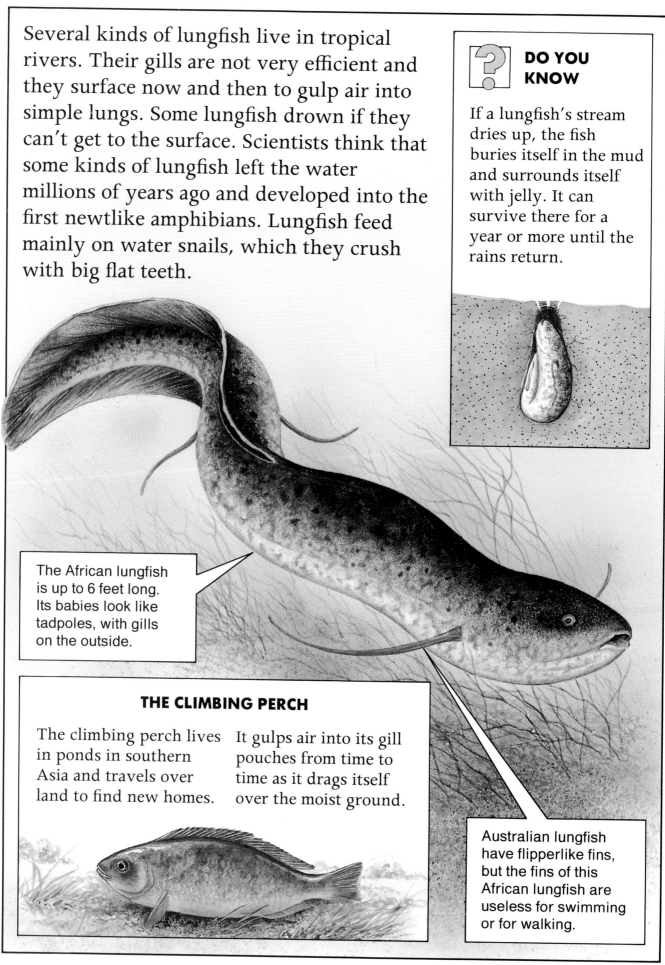

? DO YOU KNOW

If a lungfish's stream dries up, the fish buries itself in the mud and surrounds itself with jelly. It can survive there for a year or more until the rains return.

The African lungfish is up to 6 feet long. Its babies look like tadpoles, with gills on the outside.

Australian lungfish have flipperlike fins, but the fins of this African lungfish are useless for swimming or for walking.

THE CLIMBING PERCH

The climbing perch lives in ponds in southern Asia and travels over land to find new homes. It gulps air into its gill pouches from time to time as it drags itself over the moist ground.

How does the archerfish shoot its prey?

The archerfish shoots at insects sitting on leaves hanging over the water. It can spot small flies as much as 6 feet above the surface, and knocks them down with a stream of water droplets fired from its mouth. The fish then snaps them up and eats them. The archerfish is about a foot long.

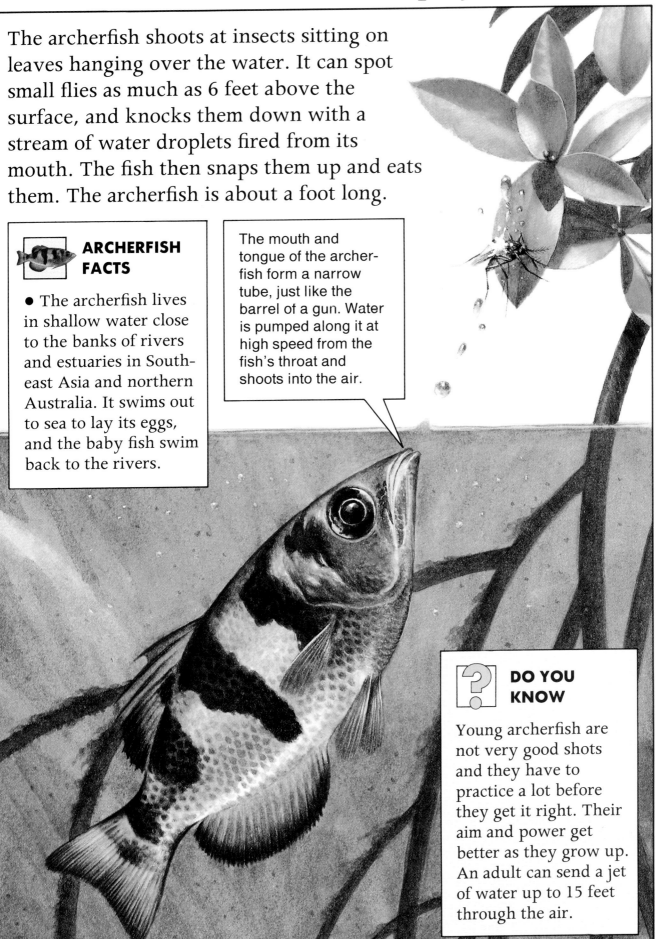

ARCHERFISH FACTS

● The archerfish lives in shallow water close to the banks of rivers and estuaries in Southeast Asia and northern Australia. It swims out to sea to lay its eggs, and the baby fish swim back to the rivers.

The mouth and tongue of the archerfish form a narrow tube, just like the barrel of a gun. Water is pumped along it at high speed from the fish's throat and shoots into the air.

DO YOU KNOW

Young archerfish are not very good shots and they have to practice a lot before they get it right. Their aim and power get better as they grow up. An adult can send a jet of water up to 15 feet through the air.

When do sticklebacks leave home?

Most fish simply scatter their eggs in the water, but the stickleback builds a cozy nest for its eggs. The father does all the work, and then guards the eggs and babies. The young fish leave when they are about two weeks old. If a baby swims away before this, the father dashes after it, grabs it in his mouth, and spits it back into the nest.

STICKLEBACK FACTS

● Sticklebacks get their name for the sharp spines on their backs. The fish in the picture are three-spined sticklebacks. They grow to about 3 inches long and are very common in ponds and streams.

1. The male builds his nest in the spring with bits of plant. He chases other male sticklebacks away from his territory.

2. The male develops bright red courting colors and uses them to attract the attention of a plump, egg-filled female.

3. The male guides the female into his nest. He taps her with his snout and she lays her eggs before swimming away.

How much food can an osprey carry?

The osprey is a fish-eating bird of prey. It catches its fish in the sea as well as in fresh water. It can carry fish weighing over 3 pounds—as heavy as the bird itself. Ospreys are great travelers and birds breeding in northern areas fly thousands of miles to spend the winter in warmer regions. They use the same treetop nests every year.

SURVIVAL WATCH

Ospreys have become rare birds in some places through people taking their eggs. Bird watchers have now started to guard the nest sites so the ospreys can rear their chicks in safety.

Broad wings provide the power necessary to lift a large fish into the air and to fly back to the nest with it.

Rough scales on the osprey's toes help them to get a good grip on a slippery fish as they snatch it from the water.

Why does the salmon make a risky journey?

The salmon spends much of its life in the sea, but it lays its eggs in the upper parts of rivers. Its journey up the river from the sea is long and dangerous and often involves leaping up waterfalls. The journey might take several months, but the salmon eats hardly anything during this time. Another amazing thing is that it always returns to the river in which it was born. Scientists think that it remembers the smell of its own river. Most salmon die after breeding, but some go back to the sea and may breed again.

SALMON FACTS

● Adult salmon grow to 3 feet long and weigh up to 70 pounds.

● Atlantic salmon often swim more than 1,200 miles to Greenland, and spend up to four years in the sea. Then they return to breed in their home rivers.

Salmon can jump as much as 10 feet out of the water and can easily leap over small waterfalls as they travel upstream.

A SALMON GROWS UP

A baby salmon is called an alevin. It is born with its own supply of food in a special pouch.

When it is about a year old, the young salmon gets red spots on its sides and is called a parr.

At about 6 inches long, the fish becomes a silvery smolt. It is now ready to go down to the sea.

Alevin

Parr

Smolt

Salmon usually reach their breeding areas in late summer. The males are bright red by this time.

The male salmon develops a strongly hooked jaw in the breeding season.

The female lays her eggs in a hollow, which she makes by flicking gravel away with her tail.

What are flamingo nests made of?

The flamingo is a really strange bird. It is up to 5 feet high and seems to be all legs and neck. It lives in shallow, muddy lakes and feeds with its head completely upside down. Flamingos live in warm areas and are most common in Africa. Thousands of them live together in enormous pink flocks. Their nests are made of mud and look just like round cakes. Each nest has a single egg sitting in a hollow on the top.

The flamingo always flies with its neck straight and its long legs trailing behind. It looks like a colorful glider.

Flamingos get their delicate color from the red pigments in the little shrimps that they eat.

The flamingo is very good at balancing on one leg. Its legs are so thin that the bird often appears to be floating in midair.

The flamingo catches shrimps and snails by sweeping its boat-shaped beak from side to side through the muddy water.

Why is the pelican's beak so large?

The pelican uses its huge beak like a bucket to scoop fish from the water. When it is fully expanded, the beak pouch can hold about 3 gallons of water. White pelicans live on lakes in many parts of the world. They are a bit clumsy on land, but they are graceful swimmers and superb fliers. They nest on the ground or in low trees.

? DO YOU KNOW

A pelican's fully out-stretched wings can be up to 10 feet across.

Baby pelicans poke their heads right into their parents' throats to get at the fish when the parents return from fishing trips.

Pelicans often swim along in a line, driving the fish into shallow water where they are easily caught.

The pelican lets the water drain out of its pouch and then gulps down any fish that it has caught.

19

Who is the otter related to?

Otters are water-loving cousins of the badger. They feed mainly on fish and leave piles of bones along the riverbank. The European otter pictured here is about 3 feet long. It makes its home in a hole in the riverbank, where the female rears two or three cubs. Otters also live on the coast and catch fish in the sea.

SURVIVAL WATCH

Otters are now rare in Europe. Fishermen used to kill them, and pollution has driven them from many rivers. Careful protection is helping them to increase again.

Otters are playful animals and they love to slide down muddy or snowy banks into the water.

The otter often uses its strong tail to prop itself upright. This helps it to see if any enemies are nearby.

A thick coat keeps the otter warm and dry even in the water. The water cannot get through the dense fur.

How do mink get into trouble?

The mink is famous for its fur, which is made into expensive coats. American mink have escaped from fur farms in Europe and have given themselves a bad name by killing all kinds of other wild animals and raiding poultry farms.

MINK FACTS

● Mink live in North America and Europe and are 2 feet long.

● American mink have the best fur and are reared on farms in many places.

The mink's feet are only partly webbed. It is a good swimmer, but not as good as its cousin the otter.

What makes the coypu valuable?

The coypu is a large cousin of the rat and comes from the rivers and swamps of South America. Coypus were taken to Europe in the 1930s and reared for their fine fur. Many escaped and became pests because they damaged riverbanks and ate crops.

COYPU FACTS

● The coypu is about 3 feet long from nose to tail. Its soft fur is called nutria.

● Coypus swim well with the help of their webbed back feet.

Why do eels return to their birthplace?

Eels are extraordinary fish. They are born way out in the middle of the Atlantic Ocean and drift thousands of miles to the rivers of North America and Europe. After a few years, when fully grown, they swim all the way back to their birthplace to lay their eggs. They do not eat on their long journey, and die soon after the eggs are laid.

EEL FACTS

● The eel grows to about 3 feet in length and weighs more than 7 pounds.

● Eels eat frogs, fish, and other creatures, but can go without food for four years.

1. Baby eels are flat and transparent. They take from one to three years to drift across the ocean to the rivers where they will live. They are 3 inches long when they arrive.

2. When the babies reach the coast they change into pencil-shaped elvers about $2\frac{1}{2}$ inches long. They swim up the rivers and eventually turn into adult eels.

3. Adult eels can survive out of water for many hours. They often wriggle over land at night to reach new lakes or streams.

Can a fish give you an electric shock?

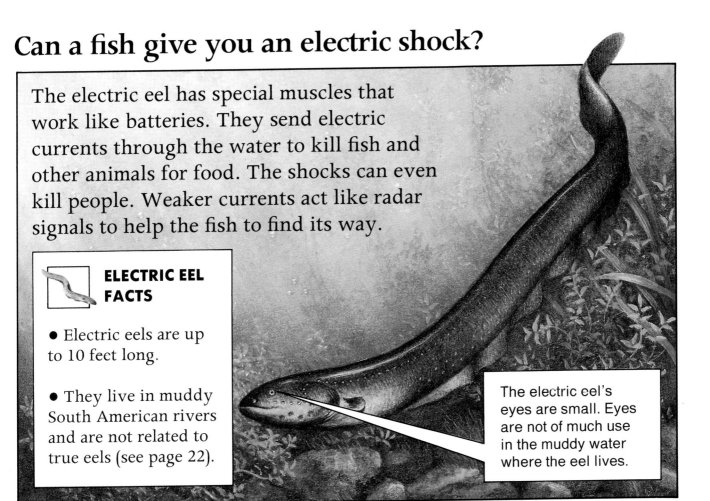

The electric eel has special muscles that work like batteries. They send electric currents through the water to kill fish and other animals for food. The shocks can even kill people. Weaker currents act like radar signals to help the fish to find its way.

ELECTRIC EEL FACTS

- Electric eels are up to 10 feet long.

- They live in muddy South American rivers and are not related to true eels (see page 22).

The electric eel's eyes are small. Eyes are not of much use in the muddy water where the eel lives.

What are a piranha's deadly weapons?

Piranhas live in the rivers of tropical South America. They feed mainly on other fish, but their strong jaws and razor-sharp teeth can quickly reduce almost any animal to a skeleton.

PIRANHA FACTS

- Some types of piranha are 2 feet long, but most are about 1 foot long.

- Amazonian Indians use piranha teeth as knives and scissors.

The piranha hunts by scent. It picks up the smell of its prey in deep pits in its snout.

What is special about a swan and its mate?

The swans shown here are mute swans, which live on ponds and slow-moving rivers in many parts of Europe and Asia. They weigh up to 40 pounds and are among the heaviest of all flying birds. Once they have paired up, the male and female swans stay together for life. Their nest is an untidy pile of twigs and leaves built among the reeds or on the riverbank. Swans feed mainly on plants, on land or in the water, but they also eat small fish and other water animals.

Mute swans have five or more babies, called cygnets, and they all stay together for several months. The cygnets do not become completely white until they are about two years old.

SURVIVAL WATCH

In Europe, many swans have died of lead poisoning after swallowing lead weights used by fishermen. The plastic weights now used mean the swans are not being poisoned, but they still get tangled up in old fishing lines.

Feathers on the ground show where the adult swans have been molting after the breeding season.

Because it is so heavy, the swan has to run across the water for up to 300 feet before it can get airborne.

DO YOU KNOW

Whooper swans and Bewick's swans breed in the far north. They fly thousands of miles in order to spend the winter in warmer places.

Most swans are white, but the native swans of Australia are all black.

Black swan

Swans feed mainly on water plants. They often put their heads and necks right into the water to reach plants on the bottom.

How do moorhens differ from ducks?

The moorhen lives on overgrown ponds and quiet streams. It looks a bit like a duck, but it does not have a flat beak. It is rather shy and is most likely to be seen swimming jerkily in and out of the reeds. When disturbed, it sounds its loud alarm call—*kuruk, kuruk*—to warn other birds. Moorhens often graze in waterside fields.

? DO YOU KNOW

The coot resembles the moorhen, but it has a white forehead. It also has a different call—*kook* instead of *kuruk*—but it is just as noisy as the moorhen.

Coot

The moorhen is not a strong flier. It has to run fast along the water surface before being able to take off.

Moorhens usually nest at the water's edge. The female lays about ten eggs. The chicks can swim when only a few hours old.

Moorhens' feet are not webbed. They cannot swim as well as ducks and spend a lot of time on land.

Which bird can run across water?

Jacanas use their long toes and claws to walk on the floating leaves of water lilies and other plants. They are also called lily-trotters. This one is the comb-crested jacana from Australia and Southeast Asia. The female jacana lays up to four shiny eggs in floating nests but it is the male who then looks after the eggs and the chicks.

JACANA FACTS

● There are seven kinds of jacana. Pheasant-tailed jacanas are the largest. They are up to 20 inches from beak to tail.

● A frightened baby jacana often hides in its father's feathers.

The jacana's slender beak picks up insects and other small animals. The bird also eats some types of plants.

The jacana's toes and claws spread its weight over several leaves, so it does not sink into the water.

How does a water spider live underwater?

The water spider lives in an air-filled tent under the water. It makes its tent with silk and fills it with bubbles of air brought from the surface. It darts out to catch passing insects and other small creatures.

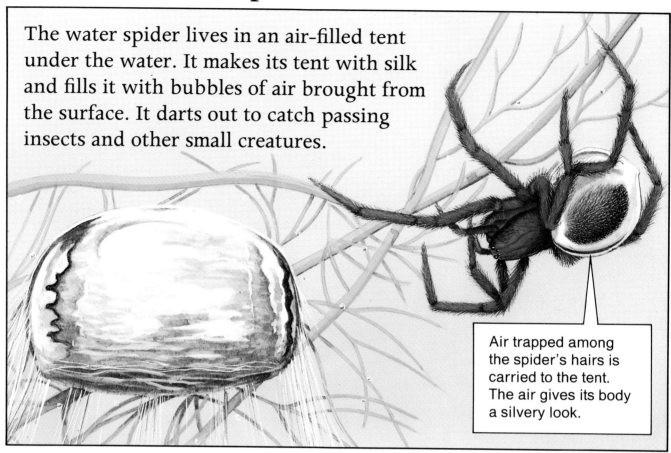

Air trapped among the spider's hairs is carried to the tent. The air gives its body a silvery look.

How does the great diving beetle move?

The great diving beetle is a ferocious pond-dwelling insect. Up to $1\frac{1}{2}$ inches long, it feeds on tadpoles and other creatures. Feathery hind legs act like oars to drive the beetle through the water. It is also a good flier.

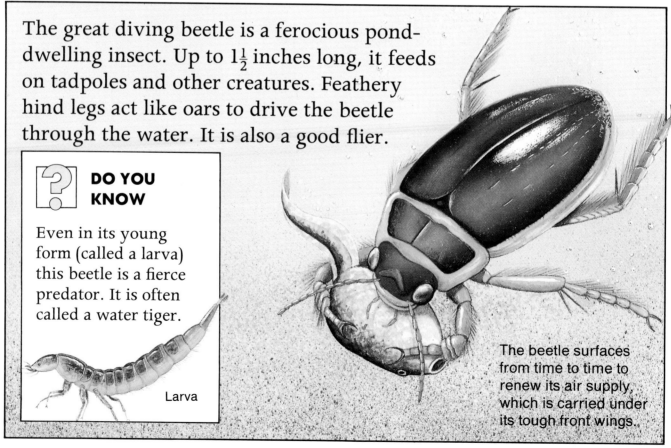

? DO YOU KNOW

Even in its young form (called a larva) this beetle is a fierce predator. It is often called a water tiger.

Larva

The beetle surfaces from time to time to renew its air supply, which is carried under its tough front wings.

How speedy is a dragonfly?

Dragonflies are among the world's fastest insects. They can zoom through the air at speeds of 20 miles per hour and can make amazing high-speed turns to snatch smaller insects in midair. Some can even hover and fly backward. Many dragonflies have regular perches and dart off from time to time to grab passing insects.

DRAGONFLY FACTS

● There are more than 5,000 kinds of dragonflies. They are also called horse-stingers, but they have no sting and are quite harmless.

The dragonfly's huge eyes, each with up to 30,000 tiny lenses, help it to spot its prey in midair.

THE LIFE CYCLE OF A DRAGONFLY

1. Dragonflies lay their eggs in water, often while still in flight.

2. Young dragonflies, called nymphs, feed on small water creatures.

3. The nymph sheds its old skin and turns into an adult dragonfly.

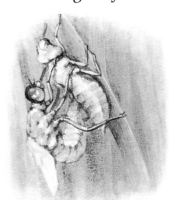

Where do newts live?

Like frogs and toads, the newt spends part of its life in the water and part on land. Newts eat lots of tadpoles and insects in the water. On land, they like damp places where they can find slugs and worms to eat. The newts shown here are warty newts, about 4 inches long.

In the mating season, the female is courted by the male. He shows off by dancing about in front of her, waving his colorful tail and crest.

 DO YOU KNOW

Baby newts are called tadpoles. They live in water and breathe with feathery gills. After three months, the tadpoles lose their gills and leave the water. They then breathe with lungs.

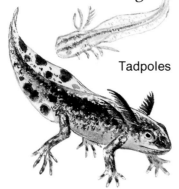

Tadpoles

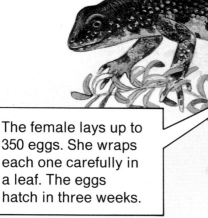

The female lays up to 350 eggs. She wraps each one carefully in a leaf. The eggs hatch in three weeks.

 SURVIVAL WATCH

Newts are rare in places where old ponds have been filled in or have become overgrown. A new backyard pond will give the newts a home and help them to survive.

How do Surinam toads hatch?

Surinam toads live in South America. When the eggs are laid, the male presses them into the female's spongy back. Each egg has its own covered pool in which it turns first into a tadpole and then into a miniature toad. Surinam toads rarely leave the water.

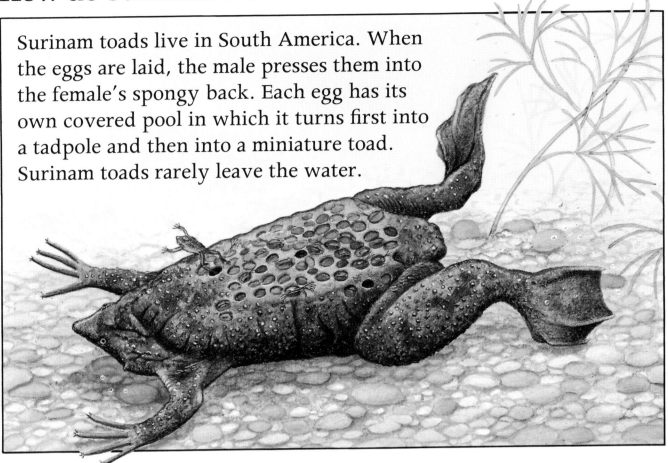

Why is the axolotl a big baby?

The axolotl is a Mexican cousin of the newt, but it does not really grow up. It stays in the water and keeps its tadpolelike look all its life, but it can still mate and lay eggs. Axolotls are up to 6 inches long. They eat small fish and other water creatures.

What makes the platypus look odd?

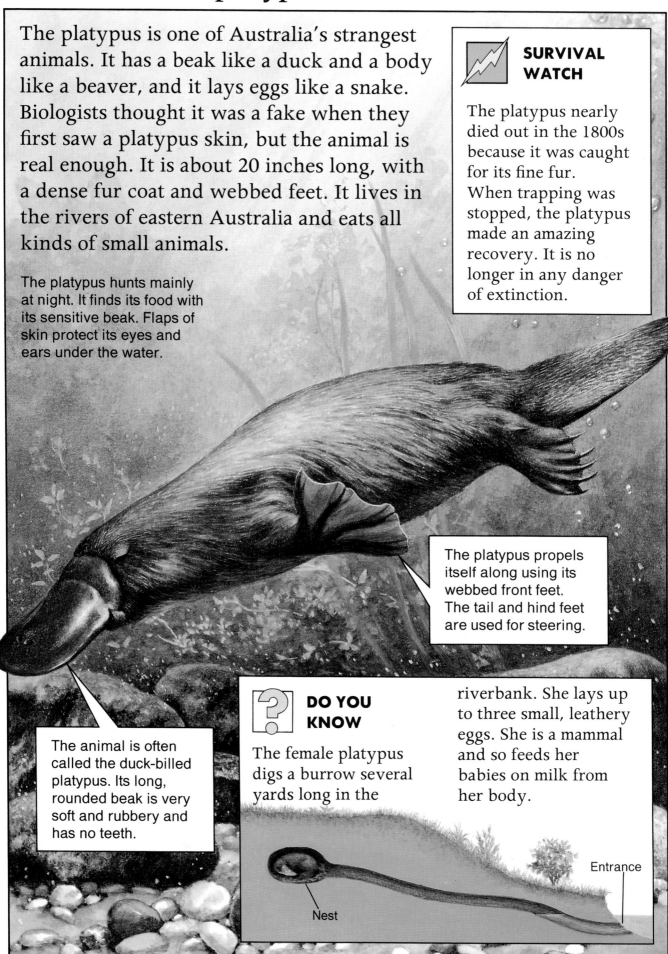

The platypus is one of Australia's strangest animals. It has a beak like a duck and a body like a beaver, and it lays eggs like a snake. Biologists thought it was a fake when they first saw a platypus skin, but the animal is real enough. It is about 20 inches long, with a dense fur coat and webbed feet. It lives in the rivers of eastern Australia and eats all kinds of small animals.

The platypus hunts mainly at night. It finds its food with its sensitive beak. Flaps of skin protect its eyes and ears under the water.

SURVIVAL WATCH

The platypus nearly died out in the 1800s because it was caught for its fine fur. When trapping was stopped, the platypus made an amazing recovery. It is no longer in any danger of extinction.

The platypus propels itself along using its webbed front feet. The tail and hind feet are used for steering.

The animal is often called the duck-billed platypus. Its long, rounded beak is very soft and rubbery and has no teeth.

? DO YOU KNOW

The female platypus digs a burrow several yards long in the riverbank. She lays up to three small, leathery eggs. She is a mammal and so feeds her babies on milk from her body.

Nest

Entrance

What does the grebe use for its nest?

The great crested grebe gets its name for the eye-catching crest of feathers on its head in the breeding season. It swims, dives, and flies well, but it is rather clumsy on land because its legs are very far back and it can't balance very well. Grebes eat small fish and other water-dwelling animals. Their nests are piles of rotting leaves floating in the water.

GREBE FACTS

● The crested grebe is 20 inches long.

● It lives on lakes and ponds in many parts of the world, but often spends the winter on the coast.

● It can swim under-water for up to three minutes, at speeds of over 6 miles per hour.

Male and female are alike. During court-ship, they dance around each other, with pieces of water plant in their beaks.

Baby grebes can swim as soon as they hatch from their eggs, but often ride on their parents' backs during the first few weeks.

How many teeth do crocodiles have?

Crocodiles are the world's largest living reptiles and they are very dangerous creatures. Several different kinds live in and around the tropical rivers. The ones pictured here are Nile crocodiles from Africa. They feed mainly on fish, but the biggest ones catch the antelope and zebras that come to drink from the rivers. Their long jaws, armed with 66 teeth, quickly tear their victims to pieces.

CROCODILE FACTS

● Crocodiles are up to 20 feet long. Some probably live for over 100 years.

● Crocodiles are the nearest living relatives of the great dinosaurs that roamed the Earth millions of years ago.

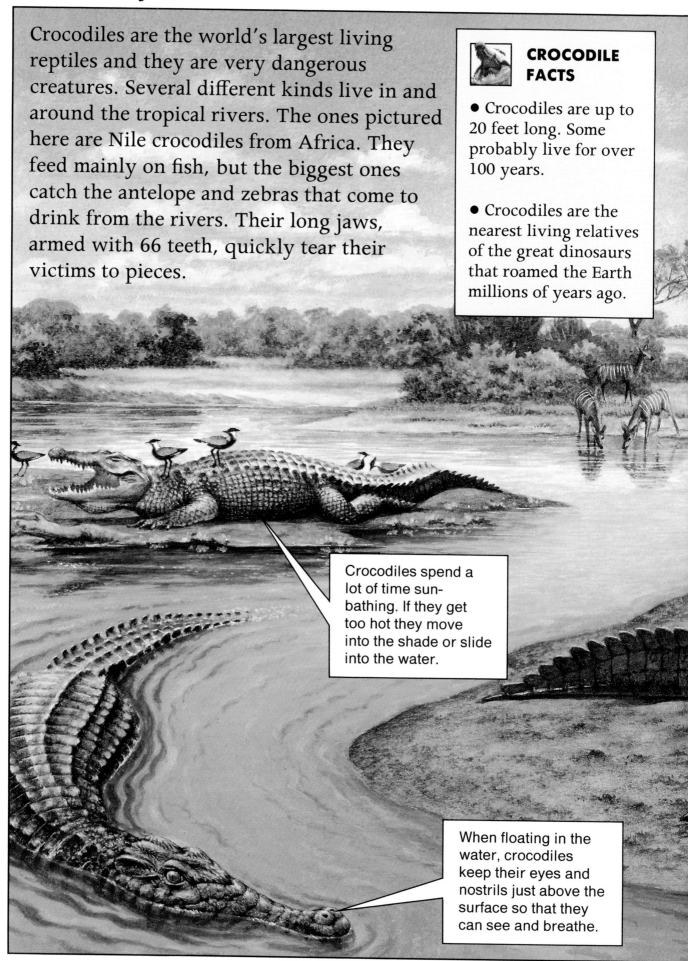

Crocodiles spend a lot of time sun-bathing. If they get too hot they move into the shade or slide into the water.

When floating in the water, crocodiles keep their eyes and nostrils just above the surface so that they can see and breathe.

DO YOU KNOW

Crocodiles lay leathery eggs. Newly hatched babies are about a foot long and the female carries them to a safe place. The babies live on land and feed mainly on frogs and insects. Later they move into the water and eat fish.

A crocodile usually slithers along on its belly, but it can also lift itself up on its legs and walk.

SURVIVAL WATCH

Crocodile skin shoes and handbags became popular about 100 years ago, and so many crocodiles were killed for their skins that they disappeared entirely from some areas. Trade in crocodile skin has now been banned, but many crocodiles are still being killed.

Plovers often enter crocodiles' mouths to peck blood-sucking leeches from their gums. The crocodiles don't harm the birds.

How does a kingfisher swallow its food?

The kingfisher fishes in shallow streams and pools in most parts of Europe and Asia. It usually fishes from a branch hanging over the water. Sticklebacks are its favorite food. They are swallowed whole when the kingfisher gets back to its perch. The bird has to turn them round in its beak and swallow them head first, so that their spines do not stick in its throat.

The kingfisher's eye contains droplets of red oil that act like sunglasses, so the bird is not dazzled by the bright water.

SURVIVAL WATCH

Many kingfishers die in cold winters because they can't fish in frozen streams. They also need clean water. Pollution has driven them from many rivers.

When it sees a fish near the surface, the kingfisher dives into the water to catch it. Each dive lasts less than a second.

DO YOU KNOW

The kingfisher builds its nest with fish bones in a tunnel in the bank.

A baby kingfisher eats about 150 small fish during its three or four weeks in the nest.

How does the heron make its own shampoo?

The heron is a patient fisherman. It catches fish and frogs in shallow water. After fishing, it cleans its feathers with its own dry shampoo, which it makes from small, crumbly feathers. Herons build their untidy nests close together in tall trees. They use the same trees year after year.

In flight, the heron bends its neck and pulls its head right back. It flaps its wings very slowly.

The heron often wades in the water to find food. It snatches up prey quickly in its long pointed bill.

A heron often stands for hours on one leg as it waits for prey. The head is usually pulled right down to the shoulders.

Why are some rivers in danger?

Rivers are used for all sorts of purposes. They are used for sports and relaxation, as well as for transportation. Unfortunately, we also use our rivers as dumps for sewage and other waste materials from our towns. Rivers can cope with small amounts of waste and carry it out to sea, but they can't cope with the huge amounts of waste that we produce today. Many rivers have been badly polluted by our trash and long stretches are now lifeless.

REPAIRING THE DAMAGE

Many countries are now taking action to clean up their rivers. They are trying to improve the treatment of sewage before pouring it into the rivers, and to find new ways to destroy factory waste. There have been some striking successes. The Thames river in London, for example, now holds fish that had not been seen there for many years.

WATER FOR DRINKING

We need lots of water for drinking and for industry. We can't take it from polluted rivers, so we take it out farther upstream. This means there is even less water to wash away the wastes we pour into the river.